STEP·BY·STEP

LEBANESE

Cooking

Your Promise of Success

Welcome to the world of Confident Cooking, created for you in the
test kitchen, where recipes are double tested by our team
of home economists to achieve a high standard of success.

MURDOCH BOOKS

Sydney • London • Vancouver

BASIC LEBANESE PANTRY

Lebanese food has become so popular that ingredients such as burghul and tahini, once only available at specialist Middle Eastern grocers, can now be purchased at supermarkets and health food stores.

Chick Peas: Hard, pale, yellow dried peas which are also known as garbanzos. Chick peas are essential in Lebanese cooking for such traditional recipes as Hummus and Falafel (deep fried spicy chick pea rissoles). Chick peas may be bought in dried or canned form in supermarkets or speciality shops. Dried chick peas should be soaked for at least 4 hours and preferably overnight before cooking.

Coriander: A pungent herb, it may be purchased fresh from many greengrocers. Its leaves are bright green and are serrated in shape. Store in a glass of water in the refrigerator, covered with a plastic bag.

Coriander may also be purchased as seeds or a ground dry powder. Store in an airtight container and use within 6 months.

Cracked Wheat (Burghul): Usually steamed until partly cooked and then crushed. Cracked wheat needs to be soaked for 10 minutes and drained well before using in salads such as Tabbouleh or in meat koftas. Store cracked wheat in an airtight container in a cool, dark place for up to 6 months.

Cumin: A spice with a warm, pungent taste, it may be bought as a seed or powder. Seeds keep their flavour longer than the ground form. For best results, grind seeds as needed. Store both types of cumin in an

airtight container.

Filo Pastry: Usually bought ready-made from supermarket freezers or refrigerated cabinets. This pastry is paper thin and is made from high gluten flour, oil and water. Filo pastry dries and cracks very quickly; cover with plastic wrap or a damp tea-towel.

Hummus: A staple food of the Middle East. It is made by grinding cooked chick peas with lemon juice, garlic and olive oil to a paste. It can be purchased ready-made in some delicatessens and supermarkets. Hummus can be served as a dip or as a sauce for kebabs.

Lentils: Available in red, green and brown varieties. Simmer for

1 hour to soften them. Lentils are often cooked until they disintegrate or they can be puréed for soups. They should be stored in dry airtight containers.

Mezze: A Middle Eastern word to describe hors d'oeuvres. Often a wide variety of mezze are served and sometimes they replace a main meal.

Okra: A green ridged vegetable pointed at one end. Can be purchased fresh from summer to autumn or bought in cans. If using fresh, trim stalk end before cooking. Store fresh in crisper of refrigerator for about 10 days. If okra is not available use zucchini or squash.

Orange Flower Water: Made from neroli, an essential oil extracted from the flowers or blossom of sweet orange trees. It is used to flavour confectionery, pastries, and sweet syrups to serve with pancakes and other Middle Eastern desserts. Can be purchased from health food stores and speciality shops.

Pistachio Nuts: Small green nuts encased in a hard straw-coloured shell. Nuts must be removed from shell (shell is opened with the hands) before eating. Store in airtight container.

Rose Water: Diluted rose essence, made from fragrant, deep-red roses.It is used in sweets, pastries and desserts to give an unusual subtle rose flavour. Can be purchased from health food stores or speciality shops.

Tahini: A brownish-grey paste made from ground toasted sesame seeds. Tahini separates on standing so stir well before using. Can be purchased in jars from health food shops, some supermarkets and speciality stores.

Yoghurt: A thick, creamy milk product made from a bacterial culture which coagulates the milk. Yoghurt is used in and served with many Middle Eastern dishes. Yoghurt has a cooling effect on the mouth and throat, so it is often served with chopped cucumber after a spicy meal. Yoghurt may be stored in the refrigerator, covered, for up to 10 days.

3

Sprinkle halved eggplant flesh with salt and stand 10-15 minutes.

Bake eggplant for 20 minutes, then peel away skin and discard.

APPETISERS (MEZZE) & SOUP

Many people order only mezze when they eat at a Lebanese restaurant, so popular are these tasty dishes.

Eggplant and Tahini Dip

Preparation time:
20 minutes
Cooking time:
20 minutes
Serves 6-8

---

2 small eggplants, halved lengthways	1/4 cup tahini
salt	1 tablespoon olive oil
2 cloves garlic, crushed	salt, to taste
2 tablespoons lemon juice	1 tablespoon finely chopped fresh mint

1 Preheat oven to 190°C.

2 Sprinkle eggplant flesh with salt. Stand for 10-15 minutes then rinse off salt and pat dry with absorbent paper.

3 Place eggplant, flesh-side-up, on a baking tray. Bake for 20 minutes or until flesh is soft. Peel off skin and discard.

4 Place eggplant flesh, garlic, lemon juice, tahini and olive oil into food processor bowl. Using the pulse action, process for 30 seconds or until smooth. Season to taste with salt.

5 Garnish with mint and serve with pita bread wedges.

Note: This dip is known as *Baba Ghannouj* and is a favourite appetiser throughout the Middle East.

Tahini is a paste made from ground toasted sesame seeds available from health food shops, supermarkets and speciality stores.

Place eggplant, garlic, lemon juice, tahini and oil into food processor.

Process the mixture for 30 seconds or until smooth. Add salt.

Hummus

The most popular
Middle Eastern dip.

Preparation time:
10 minutes +
4 hours standing
Cooking time:
1 hour
Serves 8-10

*1 cup chick peas
3 cups water
1/4 cup lemon juice
1/4 cup olive oil
2 cloves garlic,
  roughly chopped*

*2 tablespoons water,
  extra
1/2 teaspoon salt
ground sweet
  paprika, to garnish*

1 Soak chick peas in water for 4 hours or overnight. Drain chick peas, place in a pan, add water and bring to the boil. Simmer, uncovered for 1 hour, drain.
2 Place chick peas, lemon juice, oil, garlic, water and salt into food processor bowl and using the pulse action process for 30 seconds or until smooth. Sprinkle with paprika and serve as a dip with pita bread.

HINT
Add ¾ cup tahini to hummus for traditional variation *(Hummus bi Tahini)*. Stir through a little extra water to make sauce for kebabs.

Soak chick peas in water for at least 4 hours, then drain.

Cover chick peas with water, bring to the boil then simmer for 1 hour.

Process chick peas, lemon juice, olive oil, garlic, water and salt.

The hummus must be processed until it is quite smooth.

Lamb and Filo Fingers

Preparation time:
25 minutes
Cooking time:
15-20 minutes
Makes 24

2 tablespoons olive oil	1 teaspoon ground
1 onion, finely chopped	pepper
1/3 cup pine nuts	1 x 375 g packet filo pastry (see Note)
500 g minced lamb	85 g butter, melted
1/4 cup raisins, chopped	
1 cup grated Cheddar cheese	YOGHURT SAUCE
2 tablespoons chopped fresh coriander	1/4 Lebanese cucumber
2 tablespoons chopped fresh mint	3/4 cup plain yoghurt
	1 tablespoon chopped fresh coriander

1 Preheat oven to 190°C. Line a 32 x 28 cm oven tray with baking paper.

2 Heat oil in heavy-based pan. Cook onion and pine nuts over medium heat 5 minutes until golden brown. Add lamb and cook over medium heat 5-10 minutes until well browned and almost all liquid has evaporated. Use a fork to break up any large lumps of mince as it cooks .

3 Remove from heat and cool slightly. Add raisins, cheese, coriander, mint and pepper and stir to combine.

4 Place 10 sheets of pastry onto work surface. Using a sharp knife or scissors, cut pastry lengthways into 4 strips. Brush each strip with melted butter and place them on top of each other. Put a tablespoon of lamb mixture at one end of top sheet of pastry. Fold in ends and roll into a finger shape. Repeat process with remaining filo pastry and filling.

5 Place pastries on prepared tray and brush with remaining butter. Bake for 15-20 minutes or until golden brown. Serve warm or cold with Yoghurt Sauce as a party snack or entrée.

6 To make Yoghurt Sauce: Peel cucumber, remove seeds and finely chop flesh. Mix with yoghurt and coriander.

Note: Keep unused pastry covered with a damp cloth to prevent sheets drying out. Handle pastry with care – it is delicate.

HINT

These pastries may be made in advance, wrapped carefully in foil and frozen for up to 3 months. Great as a do-ahead party idea.

Cook onion and pine nuts in oil over medium heat until golden brown.

Add raisins, cheese, coriander, mint and pepper to cooked lamb.

Cut 10 sheets of filo pastry lengthways into 4 strips.

Place a tablespoon of mixture at end of the pastry. Roll into finger shape.

Spicy Filled Cabbage Leaves

Preparation time:
30 minutes
Cooking time:
20-25 minutes
Serves 6

---

6 large green cabbage leaves

FILLING
2 teaspoons olive oil
4 spring onions, finely chopped
1 clove garlic, crushed
2 tablespoons tomato paste
1/2 cup currants
2 tablespoons slivered almonds
1 teaspoon cumin seeds

1/2 teaspoon ground cinnamon
2 tablespoons finely chopped fresh parsley
2 1/2 cups cooked long-grain rice
1 cup vegetable or chicken stock

YOGHURT SAUCE
3/4 cup plain yoghurt
1 teaspoon ground cumin
1 tablespoon finely chopped fresh mint

---

1 Preheat oven to 190°C. Brush a deep ovenproof dish with melted butter or oil.
2 Blanch cabbage leaves in boiling water for 10 seconds or until soft and pliable. Drain, remove and discard the hard stalk from the leaves. Set leaves aside.
3 To make Filling: Heat oil in a large pan. Cook spring onions and garlic over medium heat for 30 seconds. Add tomato paste, currants, almonds, cumin seeds, cinnamon, parsley and rice and stir until well combined. Remove from heat and cool slightly.
4 Place 3 tablespoons of filling on edge of one cabbage leaf. Roll into a neat parcel, folding in edges while rolling. Repeat with remaining filling and leaves. Place cabbage parcels, flap side down, in prepared dish, pour over stock, cover with lid or foil and bake for 20-25 minutes or until heated through.
5 To make Yoghurt Sauce: Mix together yoghurt, cumin and mint in a bowl. Serve cabbage leaves warm or cold with Yoghurt Sauce and garnish with sprigs of fresh mint or coriander.
Note: Make the Yoghurt Sauce just before serving.

HINT
If leaves are difficult to remove from cabbage, boil whole cabbage in water to cover for 3-4 minutes. Remove and cool slightly. The leaves should separate easily. Invert a plate on top of the cabbage parcels during baking to prevent them from falling apart.

Blanch cabbage leaves in a pan of boiling water for 10 seconds.

Add tomato paste, currants, almonds, cumin, cinnamon, parsley and rice.

Place filling along edge of cabbage leaf and roll into a neat parcel.

Place filled cabbage leaves in dish and pour over stock.

Felafel with Tomato Relish

One of Lebanon's most popular dishes world-wide.

Preparation time:
  25 minutes +
  30 minutes
  standing +
  4 hours soaking
Cooking time:
  20-25 minutes
Serves 6

FELAFEL	TOMATO RELISH
2 cups chick peas	2 medium tomatoes, peeled and finely chopped
3 cups water	1/4 medium Lebanese cucumber, finely chopped
1 small onion, finely chopped	1/2 green capsicum, finely chopped
2 cloves garlic, crushed	2 tablespoons chopped fresh parsley
2 tablespoons chopped fresh parsley	1 teaspoon sugar
1 tablespoon chopped fresh coriander	2 teaspoons chilli sauce
2 teaspoons ground cumin	1/2 teaspoon ground black pepper
1 tablespoon water	grated rind and juice of 1 lemon
1/2 teaspoon baking powder	
oil for deep-frying	

1 To make Felafel: Soak chick peas in water for 4 hours or overnight. Drain and place chick peas into food processor bowl. Using the pulse action, process for 30 seconds or until they are finely ground.
2 Add onion, garlic, parsley, coriander, cumin, water and baking powder and process 10 seconds or until mixture is a rough paste. Leave mixture to stand for 30 minutes.
3 To make Tomato Relish: Place all ingredients in a bowl and mix to combine; set aside.
4 Shape heaped tablespoons of Felafel mixture into balls. Squeeze out excess liquid using your hands. Heat oil in a deep heavy-based pan. Gently lower prepared Felafel balls on a spoon into moderately hot oil. Cook felafel one at a time on spoon for 3-4 minutes, shaking spoon slightly to prevent sticking. When brown carefully remove from oil with slotted spoon. Drain Felafel well on absorbent paper.
5 Serve hot or cold Felafel on a bed of Tomato Relish or in pita bread with Relish and Hummus.
Note: If mixture is too wet, and doesn't form easily into balls, add a small amount of plain flour.

Add all falafel ingredients to ground chick peas in food processor.

Place all Tomato Relish ingredients in a bowl and mix to combine.

Shape tablespoons of mixture into balls, squeezing out liquid.

When falafel have browned, remove from oil and drain well.

Chicken and Pistachio Balls

Preparation time:
10 minutes
Cooking time:
6 minutes
Makes 14 balls

---

375 g minced chicken
3/4 cup fresh white breadcrumbs
1/3 cup shelled chopped pistachio nuts
1 egg, lightly beaten
1/2 teaspoon ground turmeric
1/2 teaspoon ground cinnamon
1 teaspoon ground coriander
1/2 cup plain flour
2 tablespoons olive oil
lemon wedges, to serve

---

1 Place chicken, breadcrumbs, pistachios, egg and spices in a bowl and stir well to combine.

2 Shape tablespoons of mixture into balls with your hands and roll lightly in flour; shake off any excess.

3 Heat oil in heavy-based pan. Cook balls in batches over medium-high heat, turning until well browned on all sides; drain well on absorbent paper.

4 Serve with lemon wedges as finger food or with a crisp green salad as a light entrée.

Remove pistachios from their shells, prising the shells open with hands.

Combine chicken, breadcrumbs, pistachios, egg and spices.

Shape tablespoons of mixture into balls and roll lightly in flour.

Cook balls in batches in hot oil until well browned on all sides.

Spinach and Lentil Soup

Preparation time:
   10 minutes
Cooking time:
   1 hour 25 minutes
Serves 4-6

2 cups brown lentils
5 cups water
2 teaspoons olive oil
1 medium onion,
   finely chopped
2 cloves garlic,
   crushed
20 English spinach
   leaves, stalks
   removed and leaves
   finely shredded

1 teaspoon ground
   cumin
2 tablespoons finely
   chopped fresh
   coriander
1 teaspoon finely
   grated lemon rind
2 cups vegetable stock
2 cups water

1 Place lentils in a large pan with water. Bring to the boil and simmer uncovered for 1 hour. Rinse and drain. Set aside. In a separate pan heat oil; add onion and garlic. Cook over medium heat until golden. Add spinach and cook a further 2 minutes.
2 Add lentils, cumin, coriander, lemon rind, stock and water. Simmer uncovered for 15 minutes. Serve immediately.

Chop onion and coriander, crush garlic, shred spinach leaves.

Cook onion and garlic in oil over medium heat until golden.

Add shredded spinach and cook a further 2 minutes.

Add lentils, cumin, coriander, lemon rind, stock and water to pan.

Drain the soaked cracked wheat, pressing down hard with spoon.

Using a sharp knife, finely chop the flat-leaved parsley and the mint.

SALADS, VEGETABLES & BREAD

The most famous Lebanese salad is Tabbouleh, indispensable in a Felafel roll, but there are many other ways to prepare the vegetables of the Middle East.

Tabbouleh

Fresh and tart.

Preparation time:
20 minutes
Cooking time:
Nil
Serves 6-8

1 cup medium cracked wheat	*2 medium tomatoes, finely chopped*
2 cups water	*2 tablespoons lemon juice*
3/4 cup chopped flat-leaved parsley	*1 tablespoon olive oil*
3/4 cup chopped fresh mint	*1 teaspoon ground pepper*
4 spring onions, finely chopped	

1 Soak cracked wheat in water for 10 minutes, drain and squeeze remaining water from wheat in a sieve, pressing down hard with the back of a spoon.

2 Place wheat, parsley, mint, spring onions, tomatoes, lemon juice, oil and pepper in a bowl and mix to combine. Serve as an appetiser with small crisp lettuce leaves to scoop up the Tabbouleh or as a side salad to a main meal.

Note: In the mountains of Lebanon, freshly picked, sharp, young vine leaves are used to scoop up the salad.

HINT
Tabbouleh is great in pita bread with slices of your favourite meat or falafel and Hummus. Store Tabbouleh covered in plastic wrap in the refrigerator.

Cut tomatoes into very small dice and squeeze 2 tablespoons lemon juice.

Place all the ingredients in a bowl and stir to mix well.

19

Spicy Potato Salad

Preparation time:
15 minutes
Cooking time:
20 minutes
Serves 6

---

500 g baby new potatoes, halved
250 g green beans, trimmed, tailed and halved diagonally

DRESSING
1/4 cup olive oil

2 red chillies, seeded and sliced
1 clove garlic, crushed
1/4 cup chopped fresh coriander
1 tablespoon red wine vinegar
1/2 teaspoon caraway seeds

---

1 Cook potatoes in a large pan of gently simmering water for 20 minutes or until tender but still firm; drain and set aside. Blanch beans in boiling water for 2 minutes or until bright green and just tender; drain beans and set aside.

2 To make Dressing: Whisk all ingredients in a small bowl for 2 minutes or until well combined. Serve salad hot or cold. Pour over dressing no more than 5 minutes before serving otherwise the salad will discolour.

Cut new potatoes into halves and slice beans diagonally.

Cook potatoes in a large pan of water until tender but keeping their shape.

Blanch beans in boiling water for 2 minutes, then drain.

Whisk all dressing ingredients together in a small bowl.

Eggplant and Coriander Salad

Preparation time:
25 minutes
Cooking time:
6 minutes
Serves 6

2 small eggplant, halved lengthways	*1 tablespoon lemon juice*
3 small zucchini	*1 tablespoon orange juice*
2 tablespoons olive oil	*1/2 teaspoon ground pepper*
1/2 cup chopped fresh coriander	

1 Cut eggplant into thin slices. Place in a colander and sprinkle with salt. Allow to stand 15-20 minutes.

2 Using a vegetable peeler, slice zucchini thinly; set aside. Wash eggplant and pat dry with absorbent paper.

Brush both sides of eggplant lightly with olive oil and place on a baking tray.
3 Cook under a preheated grill 3 minutes on both sides or until lightly browned. Set aside until cool.
4 Place eggplant, zucchini, oil, coriander, juices and pepper in a bowl and toss to combine. Serve salad as an appetiser or as a side salad to a main meal.

Sprinkle thin slices of eggplant with salt and allow to stand in colander.

Using a vegetable peeler, peel zucchini into long, thin slices.

Grill lightly oiled eggplant for 3 minutes each side until brown.

Combine eggplant, zucchini, oil, coriander, juices and pepper.

Spinach and Nut Salad

Preparation time:
  15 minutes
Cooking time:
  2 minutes
Serves 4

---

30 English spinach
  leaves
250 g young green
  beans, cut into 3 cm
  pieces
1/2 medium onion,
  finely sliced
1/3 cup plain yoghurt
1 tablespoon lemon
  juice

1 tablespoon shredded
  fresh mint
1/2 cup chopped
  walnuts, toasted
fresh mint leaves, to
  serve
red capsicum curls, to
  serve

---

1 Rinse spinach leaves several times in cold water. Boil the spinach and beans separately in water for 2 minutes or until bright green. Drain and cool.

2 Arrange spinach, beans and onion on a serving plate.

Combine yoghurt, lemon juice and mint in a small bowl. Mix well. Pour over salad, sprinkle with walnuts and garnish with mint leaves and red capsicum curls. Serve salad as a light meal with pita bread.

Cut beans into lengths and onions lengthways into fine slices.

Place spinach in boiling water for 2 minutes or until bright green.

To make dressing, combine yoghurt, lemon juice and mint in a bowl.

Finely slice red capsicums and place in iced water to make curls.

Okra with Onions and Tomato

Preparation time:
10 minutes +
4 hours soaking
Cooking time:
1 hour 4 minutes
Serves 4

1 cup chick peas	*1½ cups tomato*
3 cups water	*juice*
1 tablespoon olive oil	*2 tablespoons red*
8 small pickling	*wine, optional*
onions	*500 g okra or 2 x*
2 cloves garlic,	*375 g cans okra,*
crushed	*drained*
4 medium tomatoes,	*1 tablespoon chopped*
peeled and chopped	*fresh oregano*
1 tablespoon lemon	*1 teaspoon ground*
juice	*pepper*

1 Soak chick peas in water for 4 hours or overnight, drain. Heat oil in medium pan; add onions and garlic. Cook on medium-high heat for 4 minutes or until golden. Add tomatoes, chick peas, lemon juice, tomato juice and wine. Simmer, covered, for 40 minutes.

2 Add okra and simmer for a further 20 minutes. If using canned okra add to tomato mixture in last 5 minutes of cooking.

3 Stir through oregano and pepper. Serve with rice as a main meal or as an accompaniment to a meat dish.

Note: Okra should be washed and a thin layer of skin removed from the conical stem at the top of the pod. To prevent it becoming slimy during cooking, Middle Eastern cooks often toss okra in vinegar (½ cup to 500 g okra), then set aside for 30 minutes and rinse the okra before cooking.

If okra is not available squash or zucchini can be used.

To peel tomatoes, pour boiling water over, then plunge into cold water.

Combine tomatoes, chick peas, lemon juice, tomato juice and wine.

Add okra to sauce, mix well and simmer for 20 minutes.

At the last minute, stir through chopped fresh oregano and pepper.

Pita Bread

Use wholemeal flour if liked.

Preparation time:
10 minutes +
40 minutes rising
Cooking time:
6-8 minutes
Makes 12

1 x 7 g sachet dried yeast	*1 teaspoon caster sugar*
1½ cups lukewarm water	*3½ cups plain flour*
	2 tablespoons olive oil

1 Place yeast, water and sugar in a medium bowl. Allow to stand in a warm place for 5 minutes or until frothy.

2 Place flour, yeast mixture and oil in a food processor and process for 30 seconds or until mixture forms a ball. If not using a food processor place ingredients in a bowl and mix with a wooden spoon or with your hand until mixture forms a smooth dough.

3 Turn dough onto a well-floured board and knead until smooth and elastic to touch. Place dough in a well-oiled bowl, cover with plastic wrap, then a clean tea-towel and stand in a warm place for 20 minutes or until dough has almost doubled in size.

4 Punch air from dough, divide into 12 equal portions. Roll each portion into a 5 mm thick round. Place on greased baking trays and brush well with water. Stand and allow to rise for a further 20 minutes. Preheat oven to 250°C.

5 If dough rounds have dried, brush again with water. Bake for 4-5 minutes. The pita bread should be soft and pale in colour, slightly swollen and hollow inside. Eat warm with kebabs or falafel or cool on wire racks and serve with salad.

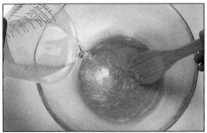

Mix together yeast, water and sugar and stand until frothy.

Process flour, oil and yeast until mixture forms a ball.

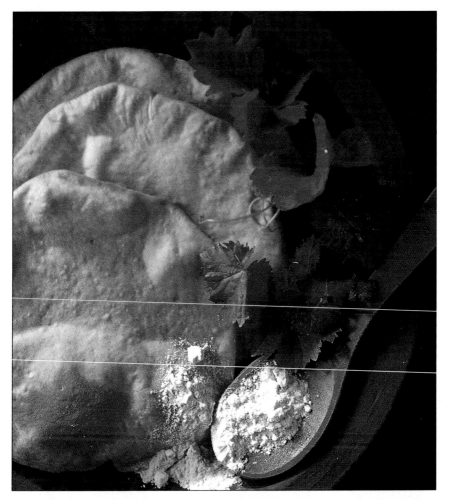

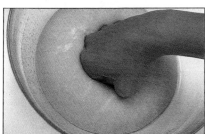

Punch air from risen dough and divide into 12 equal portions.

Roll out each portion into a 5 mm thick round and place on baking tray.

CHICKEN AND FISH

Lebanese chicken and fish dishes are light and fresh. Lemon, lime and fresh herbs are the flavourings most often used.

Grilled Chicken with Garlic and Yoghurt

Preparation time:
10 minutes
Cooking time:
8 minutes
Serves 4

4 chicken breast fillets	1 teaspoon allspice
	2 teaspoons ground
MARINADE	black pepper
1/2 cup plain yoghurt	3 cloves garlic,
1 teaspoon ground	crushed
sweet paprika	pinch cayenne pepper

1 To make Marinade: Combine ingredients in a small mixing bowl. Place chicken fillets on cold, lightly oiled grill. Spread one side with Marinade.
2 Cook under medium high heat 6 minutes or until chicken is dark brown and crisp. Repeat on remaining side. Serve with salad.

Crush garlic with salt using the flat side of a knife blade.

To make marinade combine yoghurt and spices in a small mixing bowl.

Lay chicken fillets on grill and spread one side with marinade mixture.

Turn chicken, spread uncooked side with marinade and grill until crisp.

Chicken with Lime and Spices

Fresh and healthy.

Preparation time:
15 minutes +
marinating
Cooking time:
5-10 minutes
Serves 4-6

4 chicken breast fillets	*1 teaspoon ground*
2 tablespoons olive oil	*coriander*
	1 teaspoon ground
MARINADE	*cumin*
3 tablespoons lime	*1/2 teaspoon turmeric*
juice	*1 tablespoon chopped*
	fresh mint

1 Cut chicken fillets into 1.5 cm strips. To make Marinade:

Combine ingredients in a small bowl. Add chicken strips and

marinate, covered with plastic wrap, in refrigerator several hours or overnight, turning occasionally. Drain chicken and reserve marinade.
2 Heat olive oil in a medium pan; add chicken. Cook over medium-high heat 5-10 minutes or until lightly browned and tender; stir in reserved marinade.
3 Serve chicken strips with Hummus rolled in pita bread.

Remove fat and sinew from chicken fillets and cut into 1.5 cm strips.

Combine lime juice, coriander, cumin, turmeric and mint for marinade.

Marinate chicken then drain and add to hot olive oil in pan.

Cook chicken strips until tender, then stir in reserved marinade.

Honey Mint Roasted Chicken

Preparation time:
15 minutes
Cooking time:
1 hour
Serves 4-6

---

1 x 1.6 kg chicken
2 cloves garlic,
crushed
2 tablespoons finely
chopped mint
60 g butter
juice of 1 lemon

1/4 cup honey
1 1/2 cups water
preserved ginger, to
serve
chopped almonds, to
serve

---

1 Preheat oven to 180°C. Remove excess fat pockets from chicken. Wash chicken and pat dry with absorbent paper.

2 Combine garlic and mint, spread under chicken skin. Heat butter, lemon juice and honey in a medium pan, stirring well to combine.

3 Brush chicken all over with honey mixture; tie wings and drumsticks securely in place. Place chicken on a roasting rack in a baking dish. Pour water into dish.

4 Bake 1 hour or until golden, brushing with honey mixture. Serve with preserved ginger and almonds.

Combine mint and garlic and spread mixture carefully under chicken skin.

Heat butter, lemon juice and honey and brush chicken with this mixture.

Using string, tie wings and drumsticks securely into place.

Bake the chicken for 1 hour, brushing from time to time with honey mixture.

Fish and Cumin Kebabs

Preparation time:
10 minutes
Cooking time:
5-6 minutes
Serves 4

750 g firm white fish fillets	*1 tablespoon chopped fresh coriander*
	2 teaspoons ground cumin
MARINADE	
2 tablespoons olive oil	*1 teaspoon ground pepper*
1 clove garlic, crushed	

1 Cut fish fillets into 3 cm cubes. Thread on oiled skewers and set aside.

2 To make Marinade: Combine oil, garlic, coriander, cumin and pepper in a small bowl. Brush fish with marinade. Cover with plastic wrap and store in refrigerator several hours or overnight, turning occasionally.

Drain and reserve marinade.

3 Place skewers on cold, lightly oiled grill. Cook under medium-high heat 5-6 minutes or until tender, turning once and brushing with reserved marinade several times during cooking. Serve with pita bread and seasonal vegetables.

Using firm white fish fillets, cut them into 3 cm cubes.

Place skewers in oil, then thread with fish cubes.

To make marinade, combine oil, garlic, coriander, cumin and pepper.

Grill fish kebabs, brushing them from time to time with reserved marinade.

Fish with Pine Nut Sauce

Preparation time:
   15 minutes
Cooking time:
   10-15 minutes
Serves 4

PINE NUT SAUCE	*1 cup fish or*
¾ cup pine nuts,	*chicken stock*
toasted	*1 tablespoon chopped*
2 slices wholemeal	*parsley*
bread	
1 clove garlic	*1 tablespoon butter*
1 tablespoon lemon	*rind of 1 lemon cut*
juice	*into thin strips*
	4 white fish fillets

1 To make Pine Nut Sauce: Place pine nuts, bread, garlic, lemon juice and stock into food processor bowl. Using the pulse action, process for 30 seconds or until smooth. Transfer to small pan, stir in parsley and warm through. Thin sauce with extra stock if necessary.

2 Heat butter and lemon strips in medium pan; add fish. Cook on medium heat 2 minutes each side.

3 Serve fish with Pine Nut Sauce and a green salad.

Process pine nuts, bread, garlic, lemon juice and stock for sauce.

Put sauce into small pan, stir in parsley and heat gently.

Heat butter and thin strips of lemon rind in pan.

Add firm white fish fillets and cook for 2 minutes on each side.

Baked Fish with Tahini and Chilli

Preparation time:
  10 minutes
Cooking time:
  30 minutes
Serves 4

2 x 500 g snapper	*TAHINI AND CHILLI*
1 tablespoon grated	*SAUCE*
* fresh ginger*	*½ cup tahini*
2 teaspoons ground	*1 tablespoon honey*
* sweet paprika*	*⅓ cup lemon juice*
2 onions, sliced	*½ cup water*
¼ cup water	*½ teaspoon chilli*
	* sauce*

1 Preheat oven to 180°C. Brush a deep ovenproof dish with melted butter or oil. Score each side of snapper in a diamond pattern. Rub with ginger and sprinkle with paprika.
2 Place half the onions in prepared dish. Add fish and cover with remaining onions. Add water, cover dish and bake 30 minutes or until fish flakes when tested with a fork.
3 To make Tahini and Chilli sauce: Heat ingredients until warmed through. Remove fish from dish and serve with Sauce.

Using a sharp knife, score each side of fish in a diamond pattern.

Place onions in pan, put fish on top and cover with remaining onions.

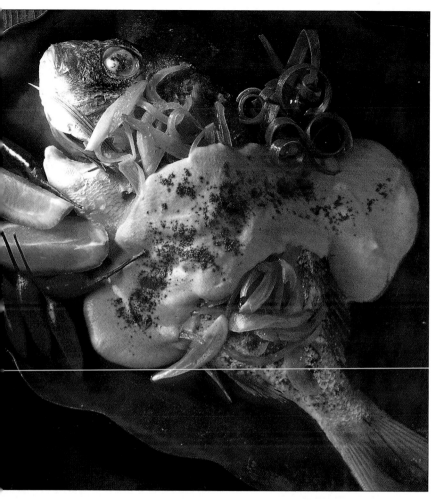

Bake fish for 30 minutes or until the flesh flakes when tested with a fork.

Combine tahini, honey, lemon juice, water and chilli sauce in pan.

Using a sharp knife make deep cuts all over the lamb flesh.

Place a slice of garlic and a piece of lemon rind into each cut.

LAMB, BEEF & VEAL

Lamb is a favourite meat in Lebanon and it is cooked in innovative ways. Beef is used less often and is usually formed into meatballs or casseroled.

Lemon and Coriander Baked Lamb

Preparation time:
15 minutes
Cooking time:
1 hour 20 minutes
Serves 4-6

1 x 1.8 kg leg lamb	*¼ cup chopped fresh*
2 cloves garlic, sliced	*parsley*
3 large strips lemon	*1 teaspoon ground*
rind cut into 1 cm	*black pepper*
pieces	*2 tablespoons olive oil*
½ cup chopped fresh	*1 cup water*
coriander	

1 Preheat oven to 180°C. Trim lamb of excess fat and sinew. Using a sharp knife make deep cuts in flesh and place a slice of garlic and a piece of lemon rind into each cut.

2 Combine coriander, parsley, pepper and oil. Coat lamb with herb mixture and place on a rack in a baking dish. Pour water into dish.

3 Bake 1 hour 20 minutes or until lamb is cooked to your liking. Add extra water to pan while cooking if it starts to dry out.

4 Serve lamb in slices with pan juices and vegetables in season.

Note: Coriander is a pungent leafy green herb, available at most greengrocers. Do not substitute dried coriander for fresh; they have quite different flavours. Water is added to pan to keep meat moist and prevent juices from burning.

Combine coriander, parsley, pepper and oil and coat lamb with mixture.

If the pan starts to dry out while lamb is cooking, add extra water.

Lamb and Eggplant Bake

Preparation time:
  30 minutes
Cooking time:
  20-25 minutes
Serves 6

---

2 eggplant, thickly
  sliced lengthways
2 teaspoons olive oil
2 medium onions,
  thinly sliced
1 kg minced lamb
1 teaspoon allspice
2 teaspoons dried
  mint leaves

2 tablespoons ginger
  marmalade
2 tablespoons tomato
  paste
1/2 cup currants
3 cups cooked
  long-grain rice
2 cups grated
  Cheddar cheese

---

1 Preheat oven to 180°C. Brush a deep ovenproof dish with melted butter or oil. Place eggplant in a colander, sprinkle with salt and allow to stand for 20 minutes. Rinse eggplant under cold water. Pat dry with absorbent paper.

2 Heat oil in a medium pan; add onions. Cook over medium heat until browned. Add lamb, cook over medium-high heat 10 minutes until well browned and almost all liquid has evaporated. Use a fork to break up any lumps of mince that form as it is cooking.

3 Add allspice, mint, marmalade, tomato paste and currants to lamb mixture. Cook for 2 minutes; remove from heat.

4 Place half the eggplant in base of prepared dish. Top with half the lamb mixture and half the rice. Sprinkle with half the cheese and repeat the layers except the cheese.

5 Cover dish and bake 20 minutes or until heated through. Remove from oven and top with remaining cheese. Place under a preheated grill for 2 minutes or until cheese is melted.

Add lamb to onions and cook until browned. Break up lumps with fork.

Add allspice, mint, marmalade, tomato paste and currants.

Place half the eggplant slices in dish and top with half the lamb mixture.

Add half the rice and sprinkle with half of the cheese. Repeat layers.

45

Spicy Lamb in Pita Bread

A good picnic dish.

Preparation time:
    10 minutes +
    2 hours marinating
Cooking time:
    10 minutes
Serves 6

MARINADE
2 cloves garlic, crushed
2 teaspoons onion powder
1 teaspoon grated fresh ginger
1 teaspoon ground pepper
1 tablespoon finely chopped fresh coriander

½ cup red wine

2 lamb loins
2 teaspoons olive oil
4 large pita breads
2 medium tomatoes, sliced
Tabbouleh, to serve
Hummus, to serve

1 To make Marinade: Combine all of the ingredients in a medium bowl. Trim lamb of any excess fat or sinew. Add lamb to marinade, toss to coat well and store covered with plastic wrap in refrigerator several hours or overnight, turning occasionally. Drain and reserve marinade.

2 Heat oil in medium pan; add lamb. Cook over medium-high heat 5 minutes each side. Add the reserved marinade during the last 3 minutes and reduce to 2 tablespoons over high heat. Slice lamb thinly.

3 Place slices of lamb on warmed, opened-out pita bread, top with tomato slices, Hummus and Tabbouleh. Roll bread to encase filling and serve immediately.

HINT
Onion powder is available in many supermarkets or where dried herbs and spices are sold. If unavailable, substitute finely grated fresh onion.

Using a sharp knife, trim lamb of excess fat or sinew.

Toss the lamb in marinade and set aside for several hours.

Drain lamb and cook in oil. Increase heat, add marinade and reduce.

Cut lamb into thin slices and serve on warmed pita bread.

Beef Koftas

Also make with lamb.

Preparation time:
20 minutes
Cooking time:
8 minutes
Serves 6

1/4 cup medium cracked wheat
1 cup water
750 g minced beef
1 small onion, finely chopped
1 clove garlic, crushed
1 teaspoon ground cumin
1/2 teaspoon ground cinnamon
1/4 cup pine nuts, finely chopped
1 egg, lightly beaten
6 pita breads, to serve
Tabbouleh, to serve

1 Soak cracked wheat in water 30 minutes. Drain. Squeeze out excess liquid. Mix with other ingredients in a medium bowl. Divide mixture into 12 equal portions.
2 Roll each portion into a sausage shape, insert a metal skewer lengthways through the middle of each.
3 Place Koftas on a cold, lightly oiled grill. Cook under medium-high heat 8 minutes turning regularly until brown and cooked through.
4 Serve in pita bread with Tabbouleh.

Mix soaked and drained cracked wheat with other ingredients.

Divide mixture into 12 equal portions and roll into sausage shapes.

Carefully insert a metal skewer lengthways.

Grill koftas under medium-high heat, turning regularly until cooked through.

Beef and Okra Stew

Preparation time:
10 minutes
Cooking time:
1 hour
Serves 6

---

2 teaspoons olive oil
2 medium onions, cut into eighths
1 kg chuck steak, trimmed and cut into 2 cm cubes
1/3 cup red wine
1/4 cup tomato paste
1 tablespoon chopped fresh coriander

8 baby potatoes, quartered
2 cups beef stock
1/4 cup chopped fresh parsley
350 g okra or 2 x 375 g cans okra, rinsed and drained

---

1 Heat oil in heavy-based pan; add onions. Cook over medium-high heat until well browned. Add meat in small batches and cook 2-3 minutes, stirring, until browned on all sides. Once all meat is browned, return it to the pan.

2 Add wine, tomato paste and coriander to pan. Cover and simmer 35 minutes. Add the potatoes and beef stock and simmer, uncovered, for 15 minutes.

3 Stir through parsley and okra and simmer for 10 minutes. If using canned okra add to stew in last 5 minutes of cooking.

4 Serve stew with bread and rice or extra vegetables.

Note: If okra is unavailable, use squash or zucchini cut into 3 cm lengths. To prepare fresh okra, lightly peel the conical stem attached to the pod. Sprinkle with vinegar and leave to stand for 30 minutes, then rinse and drain. Okra has a delicious taste but a slightly slimy texture. Marinating them in vinegar helps reduce this and makes for a crunchier texture.

Add meat to onions in small batches and cook until well browned.

Add wine, tomato paste and coriander to cooked meat in pan.

Add quartered potatoes and stock and simmer for 15 minutes.

Add parsley and okra; stir well and simmer for 10 minutes.

Meatballs in Yoghurt Sauce

Preparation time:
20 minutes
Cooking time:
15 minutes
Serves 4

---

750 g minced beef
1 medium onion,
finely chopped
1 tablespoon chopped
fresh dill
1/2 teaspoon ground
cardamom
1 teaspoon ground
cumin
2 tablespoons olive
oil

YOGHURT SAUCE
2 cups plain yoghurt
1 tablespoon
cornflour dissolved
in 1 tablespoon
water
2 tablespoons fresh
coriander leaves
1 teaspoon cumin
seeds

---

1 Combine mince, onion, dill, cardamom and cumin in a medium bowl. Shape tablespoons of the mixture into balls.
2 Heat oil in heavy-based pan; add meatballs. Cook over medium-high heat 5-10 minutes turning frequently to brown all sides. Drain on absorbent paper and set aside.
3 To make Yoghurt Sauce: Place yoghurt and cornflour mixture in a large pan and whisk until smooth. Simmer, stirring constantly for 5 minutes or until yoghurt begins to thicken. The addition of the cornflour mixture will prevent yoghurt curdling.
4 Add meatballs to Yoghurt Sauce and simmer for a further 5 minutes or until heated through. Stir in coriander and cumin seeds. Serve meatballs with an onion salad or in warmed pita bread.
Note: These meatballs can also be made with lean minced lamb. In this case, replace the coriander leaves in Yoghurt Sauce with fresh mint.

Combine ingredients in a bowl and shape into balls with your hands.

Cook meatballs in oil, turning frequently until browned all over.

Yoghurt Sauce is simmered for 5 minutes until thickened.

Add meatballs to Yoghurt Sauce, stir in coriander and cumin seeds.

Baked Veal with Spicy Chicken Stuffing

Preparation time:
  15 minutes
Cooking time:
  1 hour 30 minutes
Serves 6

---

1 x 1.8 kg shoulder veal, boned
1 tablespoon olive oil

SPICY STUFFING
2 teaspoons olive oil
6 spring onions, finely chopped
500 g minced chicken
1 cup fresh wholemeal breadcrumbs
1 teaspoon grated fresh ginger

2 red chillies, seeded and chopped
2 eggs, lightly beaten
1/3 cup chopped pecans
1/2 teaspoon ground black pepper
1/4 teaspoon paprika
1/2 teaspoon ground coriander
olive oil, extra

---

1 Preheat oven to 180°C. Trim veal of excess fat and sinew. Place flesh-side-up on a board. Butterfly thicker parts of meat; pound to flatten.

2 To make Spicy Stuffing: Heat oil in heavy-based pan; add onions and chicken mince and cook over medium heat for 4 minutes until brown.

Use a fork to break up any lumps.

3 Remove from heat, add remaining ingredients except extra oil. Stir to combine. Place mixture into food processor bowl and process 30 seconds or until fairly smooth. Spread Spicy Stuffing over veal, roll and tie up securely with string. Brush well with olive oil and place on a roasting rack in a baking dish. Pour 1½ cups water into dish.

4 Bake 1 hour 30 minutes or until cooked to your liking. Add extra water to pan as necessary and skim fat from surface. Serve with pan juices.

Cook minced chicken until brown, breaking up lumps with a fork.

Add remaining stuffing ingredients to chicken and stir to combine.

Spread stuffing over veal and roll and tie up securely with string.

Brush veal with olive oil, place on a roasting rack and bake.

Add yoghurt, milk and eggs to dry ingredients in mixing bowl.

Pour cake mixture into prepared tin and bake for 1 hour.

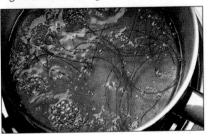

Stir Lemon Syrup ingredients over low heat until sugar dissolves.

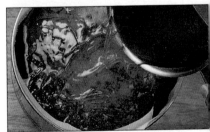

Pour half Lemon Syrup over cake as soon as it is removed from oven.

DESSERTS & BAKING

The Lebanese like their desserts sweet – they are often perfumed with rose water or orange flower water. Honey and nuts are a feature too.

Yoghurt Cake with Lemon Syrup

Preparation time:
20 minutes
Cooking time:
50-60 minutes
Serves 8-10

2¹/2 cups self-raising flour, sifted	*LEMON SYRUP*
¹/2 teaspoon baking powder	*1¹/4 cups caster sugar*
1 cup caster sugar	*³/4 cup water*
1 cup plain yoghurt	*rind of 1 lemon cut into thin strips*
1 cup milk	*¹/4 cup lemon juice*
2 eggs, lightly beaten	*lemon rind, cut into strips, to serve*
	whipped cream, to serve

1 Preheat oven to 180°C. Brush a deep 23 cm round cake tin with melted butter or oil. Line base with paper; grease paper. Place flour, baking powder and caster sugar into a medium mixing bowl. Pour over combined yoghurt, milk and eggs. Using electric beaters, beat on low speed for 2 minutes or until mixture is combined. Beat mixture on high speed for 5 minutes or until mixture is free of lumps and increased in volume.

2 Spoon into prepared tin. Bake 1 hour or until skewer comes out clean when it is inserted into centre of cake. Pour over half of prepared Lemon Syrup immediately cake is removed from oven and allow to stand for 10 minutes before turning out and serving with lemon strips, extra syrup and cream.

3 To make Lemon Syrup: Place all ingredients in a medium pan, stir over low heat until sugar dissolves; do not boil. Simmer syrup for 7 minutes or until syrup is thick. Keep warm. Remove lemon strips before serving.

Note: Yoghurt Cake is usually served warm but it can also be served cold. Lemon Syrup keeps well in a covered container in the refrigerator. It makes a refreshing drink mixed with soda water or sparkling mineral water.

Rose-flavoured Apples

Preparation time:
  15 minutes
Cooking time:
  20 minutes
Serves 4

FILLING	SYRUP
½ cup chopped glacé apricots	1 cup caster sugar
2 tablespoons chopped glacé ginger	2 cups water
⅓ cup sultanas	2 teaspoons rose water
rind of 1 lime cut into strips	4 large green apples, halved crossways

1 Preheat oven to 180°C. Brush a deep ovenproof dish with melted butter or oil.
2 To make Filling: Combine ingredients in medium bowl.
3 To make Syrup: Place sugar, water and rose water in a medium pan, stir over low heat until sugar dissolves. Simmer 4 minutes then pour into prepared dish.
4 Core apples. Place tablespoons of filling into cavity. Place in baking dish, spoon syrup over apples. Cover and bake 20 minutes basting with the syrup occasionally.
5 Serve with cream.

Pour rose-flavoured syrup into a greased ovenproof dish.

Cut apples in half crossways and remove cores.

Place a spoonful of filling into the cavity of each apple.

Spoon syrup over apples; continue basting with syrup during cooking.

Pancakes with Orange Syrup

Preparation time:
    20 minutes
Cooking time:
    30 minutes
Serves 6

PANCAKES	ORANGE SYRUP
2 cups self-raising flour	*1 cup caster sugar*
1/2 teaspoon baking powder	*3/4 cup water*
2 tablespoons caster sugar	*1 tablespoon lemon juice*
1 1/2 cups milk	*1 tablespoon orange flower water*
1/2 cup water	
1 egg, lightly beaten	

1 To make Pancakes: Sift flour, baking powder and caster sugar into a medium bowl. Make a well in the centre. Add combined milk, water and egg gradually. Beat until all liquid is incorporated and batter is free of lumps. Pour mixture into a jug and store in the refrigerator, covered with plastic wrap, for about 15 minutes.
3 When ready to cook, pour 2-3 tablespoons of batter onto lightly greased crêpe pan; swirl evenly over base.
4 Cook over medium heat 3 minutes or until underside is golden and bubbles appear on the surface. Turn pancake over; cook other side. Transfer to plate; cover with tea-towel and keep warm.
5 Repeat process with remaining batter, greasing the pan whenever it starts to become dry.
6 To make Orange Syrup: Combine sugar, water, lemon juice and orange flower water in small pan. Stir constantly over low heat until mixture boils and sugar has dissolved. Reduce heat, simmer uncovered without stirring 5 minutes or until syrup has reduced and thickened slightly.
7 Remove from heat, stand 2 minutes until bubbles subside.
8 Pour syrup over pancakes and serve in small stacks.
Note: As an alternative serve pancakes as above with 300 ml of thickened cream, whipped and 1/2 cup chopped pistachios. Don't be tempted to use more orange flower water than specified in the recipe. It is highly perfumed and too much will spoil the dish. If you prefer, omit it and the lemon juice and replace both with 2 tablespoons of fresh orange juice.

Combine dry ingredients and add milk,
water and eggs gradually.

Pour 2-3 tablespoons of batter into
greased pan, swirling over base.

When bubbles appear on surface, turn
over and cook other side.

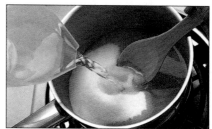

Cook Syrup in small pan until it has
reduced and thickened slightly.

61

Walnut Biscuits

Serve with coffee or as an accompaniment to ice-cream.

Preparation time:
10 minutes +
30 minutes
standing
Cooking time:
15-20 minutes
Makes 28

---

200 g butter, softened
1/2 cup caster sugar
2 tablespoons orange
  flower water
2 cups plain flour,
  sifted

WALNUT FILLING
1/2 cup walnuts,
  chopped
1/4 cup caster sugar
1 teaspoon
  cinnamon

---

1 Preheat oven to 160°C. Brush a 32 x 28 cm biscuit tray with melted butter or oil, line base with paper; grease paper.
2 Beat butter and sugar in small mixing bowl until light and creamy. Transfer mixture to a large bowl. Using a metal spoon fold in orange flower water and flour until well combined. Press with your hands until mixture comes together to make a stiff dough.
4 To make Filling: Combine all ingredients in a medium bowl and mix together well. Roll heaped tablespoons of dough into balls. Press a hollow in the centre with your thumb. Place 1 teaspoon of prepared Filling into each hollow. Place on prepared trays, flatten slightly without folding dough over filling and bake 15-20 minutes or until biscuits are golden.
5 Cool on a wire rack and serve after dinner with coffee.

Note: Orange flower water is a fragrant liquid used to flavour syrups and pastries all through the Middle East. It is available from health food shops and Greek and Lebanese grocers.

Beat butter and sugar with electric mixers in small bowl until light.

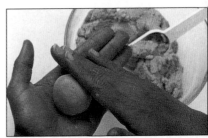

Roll heaped tablespoons of biscuit dough into balls with your hands.

Press a hollow in the centre of each ball and spoon in filling.

When biscuits are golden, remove from oven and cool on a wire rack.

INDEX